Great Gunfighters
OF THE WILD WEST

Twenty courageous Westerners who
struggled with right and wrong,
good and evil, law and order

Bill O'Neal

EAKIN PRESS ⚜ Fort Worth, Texas
www.EakinPress.com

*For
Melissa Locke Roberts—
with heartfelt gratitude
to the gifted editor
who has tactfully and
expertly improved so
many of my books.*

Copyright © 2001
By Bill O'Neal
Published By Eakin Press
An Imprint of Wild Horse Media Group
P.O. Box 331779
Fort Worth, Texas 76163
1-817-344-7036
www.EakinPress.com
ALL RIGHTS RESERVED
1 2 3 4 5 6 7 8 9
ISBN-10: 1-68179-059-0
ISBN-13: 978-1-68179-059-6

Contents

Gunfighting in the Wild West 1

Western Lawmen. 3
    Ben Thompson 5
    Wild Bill Hickok 7
    Wyatt Earp 11
    Doc Holliday 17
    Pat Garrett 19
    Bat Masterson 23
    Dallas Stoudenmire 27
    Heck Thomas 31
    John Hughes 35
    Harry Wheeler 39
    Jim Roberts 43

Western Outlaws. 45
    Jesse James 47
    Cole Younger 51
    Billy the Kid 53
    Wes Hardin 59
    Harvey Logan 63

Outlaw-Lawmen 67
    John Selman 69
    Henry Brown 73

Jim Miller	77
Tom Horn	81
Western Words	85
Places to Visit	87
Bibliography	89

Gunfighting in the Wild West

Wild Bill Hickok. Billy the Kid. Wyatt Earp. Jesse James. Bat Masterson. Tom Horn. All were gunfighters. And all are preserved in the history of the Wild West.

Western gunfighters have fascinated people for more than a century. The Wild West could easily be called the most colorful and romantic period in American history. Gunfighters like Wild Bill Hickok and Billy the Kid helped make the West wild. Because they were willing to fight with guns, in their day they were considered brave as well as dangerous.

In the West during the late 1800s, guns were tools—as good or as bad as the men who used them. Buffalo hunters used guns to earn their living. Many Westerners hunted wild game to feed themselves and their families. Outlaws used their guns for evil reasons—to rob banks and trains, and to murder people. But lawmen used their guns to stop outlaws.

The struggle between lawmen and outlaws was a battle between good and evil. It was a life and death struggle that took place in towns like Tombstone and Dodge City. But the forces of law and order finally won, and the West was tamed.

Western Lawmen

Before the frontier was settled, there were many outlaws in the West. But some men were brave enough to pin on badges and fight the outlaws. For example, Sheriff Pat Garrett hunted down and killed the murderous Billy the Kid.

Lawmen such as Wild Bill Hickok, Wyatt Earp, and Bat Masterson fought to make the wild Kansas cowtowns safe. Texas Rangers, such as Capt. John Hughes, chased outlaws across the Lone Star State. Capt. Henry Wheeler led the Arizona Rangers.

Wherever they wore a badge, Western lawmen led dangerous lives. Wild Bill Hickok, Pat Garrett, Ben Thompson, and Dallas Stoudenmire were killed by

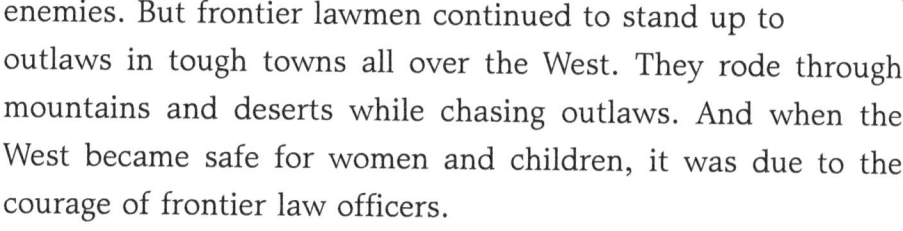

enemies. But frontier lawmen continued to stand up to outlaws in tough towns all over the West. They rode through mountains and deserts while chasing outlaws. And when the West became safe for women and children, it was due to the courage of frontier law officers.

Ben Thompson was the first important gunfighter. Ben fought in gunfights before, during, and after the Civil War. (Author's collection)

Ben Thompson
THE FIRST GREAT GUNFIGHTER

It seems a little strange that the first great Western gunfighter was born in England.

Ben Thompson, born in 1842, was the oldest son of a British naval officer. In 1851 his family moved from England to join relatives in Austin, Texas. Eight-year-old Ben would grow up on the Texas frontier.

During the 1850s, Texas was a violent land. There was little law and order in the state. Men settled their quarrels with fists and guns. And Texans defended their homes from the raids of Comanche warriors.

Ben learned that he would have to fight to protect himself and his loved ones. By the time he was seventeen, he twice had defended himself with a shotgun against other teenagers. Ben was wounded once, but during both quarrels he wounded his opponent.

In 1860 Comanche raiders carried off five children from Austin. Seventeen-year-old Ben joined the pursuit. The Comanches ambushed their pursuers, but Ben shot the chief, and the five children were rescued.

Ben went to New Orleans to work at a printer's shop. When a thief tried to steal items from the shop, Ben found a gun and wounded him.

Ben soon returned to Texas. When the Civil War started, he joined the Confederate Army to defend his home. But the South lost the war and was then policed by U.S. troops. Texans hated being told what to do by Northern soldiers. Ben and some of his friends fought with the soldiers, and two soldiers were killed.

In Austin, Judge Julius Schuetze was attacked by five men with knives. Ben saw the attack and chased the men away with his pistol.

Ben married a woman named Catherine Moore. Her brother, James Moore, mistreated Ben's mother. Then James hit Catherine. To protect his wife and mother, Ben shot and wounded James.

During the 1870s, Ben spent a few years in the Kansas cattle towns. In rip-roaring Abilene he ran the Bull's Head Saloon. In Dodge City he joined his friend, Bat Masterson. Then Ben went to Colorado, where a railroad paid him $5,000 to protect their property. Eventually, Ben returned to Austin. Once more he had to ride with other Texans against Comanches.

On Christmas night of 1876, Ben attended a show in an Austin theater. The owner of the theater, Mark Wilson, quarreled with Ben. When Wilson tried to shoot Ben with a shotgun, Ben pulled his six-gun and shot Wilson three times. Wilson's friend, Charles Mathews, shot Ben in the hip. Ben fired back, and his bullet knocked out some of Mathews' teeth.

Ben surrendered to lawmen. A jury later released him because he had fought in self-defense.

Many times Ben had fought to protect his family or friends in Austin. People in Austin trusted and admired him. In 1881 they elected him city marshal. Ben was an excellent peace officer.

The next year Ben visited San Antonio. At the Vaudeville Theatre Ben met an old enemy, Jack Harris. Harris pointed a shotgun at Ben. Ben answered with his six-gun, shooting Harris in the chest.

Harris died that night. As a result, Ben resigned as marshal of Austin. But a San Antonio jury later acquitted Ben. When he returned to Austin, his friends staged a parade for him.

In 1884 Ben met a friend in San Antonio, a deputy sheriff from Uvalde named King Fisher. Ben and King unwisely went to the Vaudeville Theatre. There, friends of Jack Harris murdered Ben and King with shotguns and rifles. Ben was shot nine times; King was shot thirteen times.

Ben had participated in fourteen gunfights and had killed six men. In all cases he had fought to defend himself or to protect others. But Ben Thompson had lived by the gun, and he died by the gun.

Wild Bill Hickok
THE PRINCE OF PISTOLEERS

Wild Bill Hickok was a big, courageous man who led a life of adventure on the frontier. He was so good with pistols that he was called "The Prince of Pistoleers."

James Butler Hickok was born in Illinois in 1837. His father was a farmer and a storekeeper. Jim's father also helped runaway slaves from the South escape to Canada. Young Jim often helped his father take slaves toward freedom in Canada.

Jim loved to hunt and to practice shooting. By the time he was a teenager, he was the best shot in northern Illinois.

Jim grew tall and strong. When he was eighteen he had a fistfight with a young man named Charlie Hudson. Jim hit Charlie so hard that he collapsed. Thinking that Charlie was dead, Jim ran away to the West. (Charlie soon recovered.)

Jim first wore a badge as constable of Monticello, Kansas. Later he was a stagecoach driver on the Santa Fe Trail. Then he was hired by the famous express company, Russell, Majors & Waddell. Jim was a wagon master for the company.

While leading a wagon train through the Colorado mountains, Jim was attacked by a bear. He killed the bear with his knife and pistols, but Jim was badly clawed. He was sent to Santa Fe and to Kansas City for medical treatment. As he recovered, his company sent him to the Rock Creek stagecoach station on the Oregon Trail in Nebraska. The station was run by Horace Wellman and by stablehand Doc Brink.

Wild Bill Hickok wore his guns with the butts forward.
(Courtesy Kansas State Historical Society)

Across the creek from the station was the ranch of Dave McCanles. McCanles and Jim began to have trouble. Because Jim had a large upper lip, McCanles insulted him by calling him "Duck Bill." Hickok grew a mustache to cover his lip, but people continued to call him "Bill."

On July 12, 1861, McCanles crossed the creek to the station. He shouted for Hickok to come outside and fight fairly. Hickok tried to avoid a fight, but McCanles came inside the station looking for trouble.

Hickok shot McCanles in the heart with a pistol. A cousin of McCanles, James Woods, and a ranch worker, James Gordon, ran toward Hickok, who opened fire and wounded both men. Woods and Gordon tried to run away but were chased down and killed by Horace Wellman and Doc Brink.

This wild fight was reported in newspapers and magazines. Hickok became famous as a fighting man.

By this time the Civil War had started. Hickok became a wagon master with the Union Army in Missouri. Later he served the army as a scout, and he had many dangerous adventures. Once he saved a prisoner from a lynch mob. A woman shouted, "Good for you, Wild Bill!" For the rest of his life people would call him "Wild Bill."

After the war, Wild Bill stayed in Missouri. In Springfield he had an argument with a gambler named Dave Tutt. Dave and Wild Bill met in the town square. A large crowd of onlookers gathered.

Dave and Wild Bill were armed with pistols. When the two men were seventy-five yards apart, Wild Bill shouted, "Don't come any closer, Dave!" Dave fired a shot but missed. Wild Bill steadied his pistol with his left hand and fired a bullet squarely into Tutt's chest. Tutt fell face down, dead in an instant.

Wild Bill moved to Fort Riley, Kansas. He served as a cavalry scout against Native American warriors. Wild Bill was given the badge of a deputy U.S. marshal, so that he could chase army deserters and thieves of army horses. In April 1868 he and his friend, Buffalo Bill Cody, rounded up eleven prisoners.

Later in the year, Wild Bill was with a group of men who were attacked by a war party. Although he was wounded in the foot, Wild Bill rode past the warriors and brought soldiers to the rescue.

In 1869 Wild Bill Hickok was elected sheriff of Ellis County, Kansas. The county seat was Hays City, and Fort Hays was nearby. Soldiers and cowboys came to the town's saloons. It came to be known as a wild and dangerous town.

Three times Wild Bill got involved in saloon brawls. Twice he had to shoot drunken soldiers. Another time he had to kill a troublemaker named Samuel Strawhim.

In 1871 Wild Bill was hired to be city marshal of Abilene, Kansas. Abilene was the first of the Kansas cattle towns. The saloons and dance halls there were filled with gamblers and Texas cowboys.

Once a gambler named Phil Coe caused trouble on Abilene's main street. Coe was backed up by a crowd of Texas cowboys. When Marshal Hickok tried to stop the trouble, Coe drew a pistol. But Wild Bill beat him to the draw. Coe dropped to the ground with a bullet in his stomach.

A man ran through the crowd toward the marshal. Wild Bill whirled and shot the man in the head. But the man was Wild Bill's deputy, who was coming to help.

Wild Bill had accidentally killed his own deputy. He was deeply troubled to realize that he had shot his friend. Wild Bill never shot at another man the rest of his life.

For a time, Wild Bill went back east. With Buffalo Bill Cody, he starred in a play about the West, *Scouts of the Prairie*. Soon, however, he returned to the West.

In 1876 he went to Deadwood, a gold-mining boomtown in the Black Hills of Dakota Territory. A man named Jack McCall wanted to kill the famous Wild Bill. McCall sneaked up behind Wild Bill while he was playing poker in a saloon and shot Wild Bill in the back of the head. Later McCall was executed for murder.

Wild Bill Hickok was dead. But the legend of the Prince of Pistoleers will live as long as the Wild West is remembered.

Wyatt Earp
LAWMAN AT THE O.K. CORRAL

Wyatt Earp was one of the most famous lawmen of the Old West. He did not like to shoot people. When making an arrest, Wyatt would hit a troublemaker with his fist or gun barrel. He would knock a man unconscious, rather than shoot him.

Wyatt's father taught him to fight with his fists. "There were few men in the West who could whip Earp in a rough and tumble fight . . . ," wrote Wyatt's friend, Bat Masterson.

Wyatt was part of a large family. The Earps were very loyal to each other. One time, in the streets of Lamar, Missouri, Wyatt and three of his brothers—James, Morgan, and Virgil—fought for twenty minutes against five other men.

In Lamar in 1870, twenty-two-year-old Wyatt Earp first wore a badge, as town constable. Later, he went west as a buffalo hunter. In 1875 he joined the police force of Wichita, Kansas. The next year, he became a policeman in another Kansas cattle town, Dodge City.

During his years as a lawman in the Kansas cattle towns, Wyatt had to use his guns only once. In 1878 in Dodge City, a few drunken cowboys began shooting their guns during the middle of the night. Wyatt and another officer tried to stop the cowboys. Then the cowboys and lawmen began shooting at each other. The cowboys rode out of town, but one of them was wounded, and he later died.

In 1880 the Earp brothers moved to Tombstone, Arizona. Wyatt,

Wyatt Earp fought in the West's most famous shootout, the Gunfight at the O.K. Corral in Tombstone, Arizona.

(Courtesy Arizona Historical Society)

James, Virgil, Morgan, and Warren Earp lived near each other in the famous mining town. Wyatt's loyal friend, Doc Holliday, also moved to Tombstone.

Wyatt became a deputy sheriff of Cochise County. Virgil became city marshal of Tombstone. The Earps began to feud with the Clanton and McLaury brothers, who led an outlaw gang. The Clantons and McLaurys were rustlers, and they also robbed stagecoaches.

The Earps tried to stop the outlaws, but the Clantons and McLaurys continued to cause trouble. Finally, on October 26, 1881, the two groups shot it out in the West's most famous gunfight.

Ike and Billy Clanton, Frank and Tom McLaury, and Billy Claiborne were at the rear gate of the O.K. Corral. Wyatt, Virgil, and Morgan Earp, along with Doc Holliday, marched toward the outlaws.

Wyatt considered Frank McLaury the best gunfighter on the outlaw side. If a fight started, Wyatt intended to try to shoot Frank first.

Marshal Virgil Earp wanted to arrest the five men. "Throw up your hands," he ordered. Suddenly, the street exploded with gunfire. Wyatt shot Frank McLaury in the stomach. Virgil shot Billy Clanton. Doc killed Tom McLaury with a shotgun blast. Ike Clanton and Billy Claiborne ran away.

Frank McLaury and Billy Clanton, although badly wounded, continued to fire their six-guns. Virgil took a bullet in the leg. Morgan was hit in the neck, while Doc was grazed in the side.

But the Earps continued to shoot. Billy was hit and hit again. Frank was shot in the head. Billy Clanton and Frank and Tom McLaury died at the O.K. Corral. But everyone on the Earp side recovered.

Virgil Earp was shotgunned from ambush after the O.K. Corral shootout.
(Courtesy Arizona Historical Society)

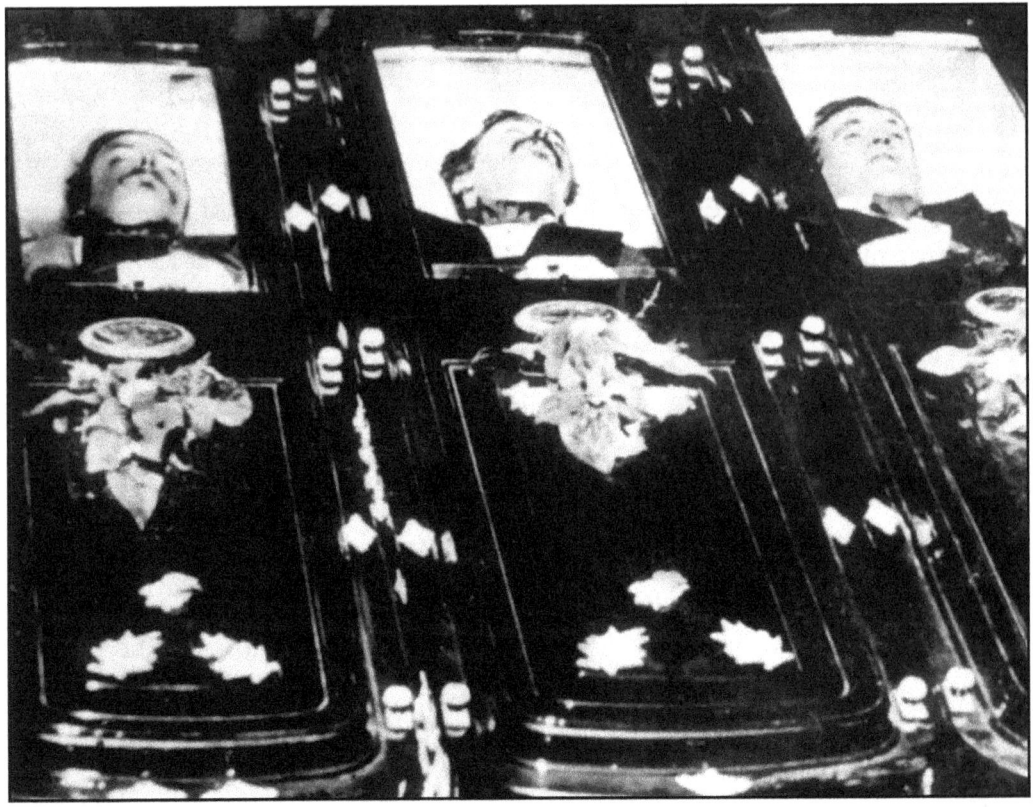

Left to right: Tom McLaury, Frank McLaury, and Billy Clanton, all killed at the O.K. Corral.

(Courtesy Western History Collections, University of Oklahoma Library)

Outlaws wanted revenge against the Earps. Two months after the O.K. Corral gunfight, Marshal Virgil Earp was ambushed on Tombstone's main street. A shotgun blast crippled his left arm.

"Never mind," Virgil bravely told his wife, "I've still got one arm left to hug you with."

A few months later, Morgan Earp was shot in the back while playing pool. Another bullet narrowly missed Wyatt. As he lay dying, Morgan told Wyatt, "This is the last game of pool I'll ever play."

Wyatt intended to make the outlaws pay for shooting his brothers. Doc Holliday would help. So would Warren Earp, Wyatt's youngest brother. Also helping Wyatt were two friends, Sherman McMasters and "Turkey Creek" Jack Johnson.

These dangerous men put Morgan's body on a train in Tucson. Virgil, still recovering from his wound, would take Morgan to the family home in California.

One of the murder suspects, Frank Stilwell, was at the Tucson depot. Stilwell may have been attempting another ambush. Wyatt and his men chased him down. Stilwell was shot to death.

Two days later, Wyatt and his men rode after another murder suspect, Florentino Cruz. They found Cruz in the country near Tombstone. Like Stilwell, Cruz was shot dead. There were rumors that other outlaws were killed by Wyatt.

Now that the deaths of his brothers were avenged, Wyatt left Arizona. He visited Colorado, Idaho, Wyoming, Nevada, Texas, and California. Wyatt returned to Dodge City to help his friend, Luke Short, with a problem. He refereed a heavyweight championship boxing match during this time. Later he spent four years in Alaska during the gold rush.

After Wyatt died, books were written about him and his brothers and Doc Holliday. There was a television series about Wyatt Earp, and many movies were filmed about the O.K. Corral shootout. As long as people remember the Old West, the story of Wyatt Earp will be told.

Doc Holliday sometimes served the law when helping his friend, Wyatt Earp.
(Courtesy Kansas State Historical Society)

Doc Holliday
THE DEADLY DENTIST

One of the most fascinating gunfighters of the Old West was Doc Holliday. When he was a young man, he learned that he had tuberculosis. There was no cure for this lung disease during the 1800s. Doctors told him that he would live longer in the dry climate of the West.

In the West, Doc remained sick. He knew he would die after a long illness. So it didn't bother him to get involved in fights, using guns and knives. It seemed that Doc hoped he would be killed. But no one could kill him. Finally, Doc began to use his guns on the side of law and order, helping his friend, Wyatt Earp.

John H. Holliday was born in Georgia in 1851. He was raised in the Old South. He dressed well and had the manners of a Southern gentleman.

He studied in Philadelphia to become a dentist. Doc opened an office in Atlanta, Georgia. His mother had died of tuberculosis, and soon Doc was suffering with the deep cough of a tuberculosis victim.

In 1873 Doc went west, seeking a drier climate. He opened a dentist's office in Dallas, Texas, but being in the West made him more adventurous. He began to gamble and drink in saloons. On New Year's Day of 1875, Doc and a Dallas saloonkeeper had an argument. They shot at each other, but no one was hurt.

Doc began to travel from one Western boomtown to another. He went from Dallas to the wild buffalo hunter's town near Fort Griffin. He went to such Colorado mining towns as Denver and Leadville. Doc also traveled to Cheyenne, Wyoming.

In 1878 Doc opened a dentist's office in the famous Kansas cattle town of Dodge City. In Dodge, Doc met Assistant City Marshal Wyatt Earp. Unlike Doc, Wyatt was tall and strong. Doc greatly admired Wyatt.

Once, when Wyatt was threatened by several enemies, Doc came to his rescue. Wyatt and Doc became close friends. Doc was always ready to help Wyatt. When Wyatt moved to Tombstone, Arizona, his friend soon followed.

In Tombstone, Wyatt and his brothers opposed a gang of rustlers led by the Clanton and McLaury families. Virgil Earp was city marshal of Tombstone when the trouble came to a head: Virgil was backed by his brothers, Wyatt and Morgan, and by Doc.

On October 25, 1881, Doc and Ike Clanton quarreled in a Tombstone saloon. That day the Earp brothers had other trouble with the Clantons and McLaurys. On October 26 Frank and Tom McLaury, Ike and Billy Clanton, and Billy Claiborne gathered at the O.K. Corral. The three Earp brothers and Doc walked to the corral, ready for trouble. Virgil appointed Doc a deputy city marshal.

Doc carried his revolver and a double-barreled shotgun to the O.K. Corral. When the shooting started, Doc fired his shotgun at Tom McLaury. Tom was hit by twelve buckshot. He collapsed and died.

Frank McLaury fired a pistol shot that grazed Doc in the side. But Frank was already badly wounded. Doc's shotgun was now empty. He drew his six-gun and fired at Ike Clanton. But Ike ran unharmed into a nearby building. Billy Claiborne also ran away.

The shooting stopped. Frank and Tom McLaury were dead. Billy Clanton was dying. Virgil and Morgan Earp recovered from their injuries. They were later ambushed by enemies, and Morgan died. When Wyatt went in search of the killers, Doc went with him. He helped Wyatt kill two of the murderers.

Because of all the trouble, Doc left Tombstone. He spent his last years in Colorado as a gambler. His tuberculosis grew worse, and in 1887 he died in his hotel room in Glenwood Springs. He was thirty-six.

Doc had fought in at least eight gunfights but was never seriously injured. As he lay in bed, quietly dying of tuberculosis, he said, "This is funny."

Pat Garrett
HE STOPPED BILLY THE KID

Billy the Kid was the most famous outlaw in New Mexico. When Billy was hunted down and killed by Sheriff Pat Garrett, Pat won undying fame as a frontier peace officer.

Pat was born and raised in Alabama, but he wanted adventure in the West. When he was eighteen, he moved to Texas to become a cowboy. During the next several years, Pat also worked as a buffalo hunter.

In 1876 Pat had a fight with another buffalo hunter named Joe Briscoe. Briscoe finally grabbed an ax and ran toward Pat. Pat shot him with his Winchester.

After Briscoe died, Pat left Texas and went to New Mexico. At Fort Sumner he opened a restaurant and herded cattle. Pat married and began to raise a family.

Pat Garrett was serious and hard-working. At six feet, four inches, he was an impressive man. In 1880 he was elected sheriff of Lincoln County.

New Mexico's Lincoln County was the largest county in the United States. This vast county was the scene of cattle rustling and constant violence. Lincoln County's worst outlaw was a rustler and killer known as Billy the Kid.

Pat knew Billy the Kid. His main job as sheriff was to find and arrest Billy, but the Kid had many friends who were willing to hide him.

Pat formed a posse to search for Billy the Kid and his gang. Pat and

Sheriff Pat Garrett killed the most famous outlaw in the West, Billy the Kid.
(Courtesy Arizona Historical Society)

his men rode across the countryside hunting outlaws. In one village, an outlaw named Manuel Leiva dared Pat to arrest him. Pat knocked him down. Leiva pulled a six-gun and fired at Pat. The bullet missed, and Pat shot Leiva in the shoulder.

On the night of December 19, 1880, Pat and his posse set a trap for Billy and his gang. Billy and five other outlaws rode into the trap. Billy's friend, Tom O'Folliard, was shot by Pat or a deputy. Billy and the other outlaws escaped into the darkness.

Tom O'Folliard rode slowly toward the lawmen. "Don't shoot, Garrett," he said. "I'm killed." Tom died later that night.

Pat led his posse in chasing after the other outlaws. Although the countryside was covered with snow, within four days Pat tracked the outlaws to a stone cabin.

Charlie Bowdre came out of the cabin and was shot. He staggered forward and died in Pat's arms. Later in the day Billy and the other outlaws surrendered.

Billy the Kid was convicted of murder. A judge sentenced him to hang. But Billy killed two guards and escaped from the jail.

Sheriff Pat Garrett had captured Billy the Kid once. Now Pat had to chase the dangerous outlaw again. This time Pat would take no chances.

After months of detective work, Pat found Billy the Kid in Fort Sumner. On the night of July 14, 1881, Billy walked into a dark room where Pat waited. Billy had a gun and a knife, and Pat took no chances. He shot the outlaw in the heart. Now Pat was famous as the man who had killed Billy the Kid.

When rustling became a problem in the Texas Panhandle, Pat was hired to lead a band of special rangers. He eventually returned to New Mexico as sheriff of Doña Ana County to solve a murder mystery.

Pat actually spent more years working as a rancher than as a lawman. A feud developed between Pat and another rancher, and in 1908 Pat was shot to death near his ranch in New Mexico. It was never determined who murdered the famous Pat Garrett.

Bat Masterson was elected sheriff of Ford County at Dodge City, Kansas.
(Courtesy Kansas State Historical Society)

Bat Masterson
DANGEROUS WITH GUNS OR FISTS

His real name was William Bartholomew Masterson. But he became famous as Bat Masterson. No one knows why people called him "Bat." Maybe it was short for Bartholomew. Maybe it was because he would battle anyone with guns or fists. Or maybe it was because, when he was sheriff, he batted lawbreakers on the head with a walking stick.

Bat was born in Canada in 1853. He lived with his family on farms in Canada, New York, Illinois, and Kansas. When he was eighteen, he and his older brother, Ed, left the farm.

Bat and Ed went to Dodge City. Bat soon became a buffalo hunter. On July 27, 1874, Bat and about two dozen other buffalo hunters were attacked by hundreds of Comanche warriors at a Texas trading post, Adobe Walls. Four men were killed, but the outnumbered buffalo hunters fought off the huge war party.

After the Battle of Adobe Walls, Bat worked as an army scout. In 1876, near Fort Elliott, Texas, he was attacked by a soldier named Melvin King. King shot Bat and a girl he was with. Bat shot the soldier. King and the girl died, and Bat had to use a walking stick because of his hip wound.

Soon Bat returned to Dodge City. Ed Masterson had become city marshal of Dodge. Bat became a deputy sheriff of Ford County. He was a fine law officer, and in 1877 he was elected sheriff of Ford County.

Sheriff Masterson arrested troublemakers. When a girl named Dora Hand was killed by a cowboy, Bat led a posse. They chased down and shot the cowboy.

Bat also was a deputy U.S. marshal during this period. Twice he led large groups of gunmen to protect railroad property. Sadly, his brother Ed was killed in a gunfight with drunken cowboys.

After Bat left the sheriff's office, he traveled all over the West. He was often hired to manage gambling halls. Bat kept the gamblers from causing trouble, because they knew how dangerous he was with a gun.

In 1881 Bat joined several Dodge City friends, including Wyatt Earp and Luke Short, in Tombstone, Arizona. A few years later, Bat was with Short in Fort Worth when Luke killed "Longhaired Jim" Courtright in a gunfight.

Jim Masterson was two years younger than Bat. He followed his brothers Bat and Ed to Dodge City. Jim was a law officer for more years than Bat. In 1881 Jim had a gunfight with two men in Dodge City. No one was hurt, but Jim expected more trouble. He sent a telegram to Bat in Tombstone asking for help. Bat immediately boarded a train for Dodge.

At noon on April 16, 1881, Bat stepped off the train in Dodge. Suddenly, he saw Al Updegraff and A. J. Peacock, the men who had shot at Jim. Bat shouted at Updegraff and Peacock.

"I have come over a thousand miles to settle this," said Bat. "I know you are heeled—now fight!"

Updegraff and Peacock pulled their guns and opened fire. Bat ducked for cover and returned their fire.

Jim Masterson heard the gunshots from a nearby building. He and a friend began shooting at Updegraff and Peacock. Bullets shattered windows and thumped into the walls of buildings. People on the street ran for cover. A bullet kicked dirt into Bat's mouth. Another bullet badly wounded Updegraff.

After three or four minutes, the shootists had to reload their guns. When the shooting stopped, the mayor and the sheriff marched into the

Left: *Jim Masterson was Bat's deputy sheriff in Dodge City. He also served as city marshal and as a deputy U.S. marshal. Jim fought in more gunfights than his older brother Bat.* Right: *Ed Masterson, Bat's older brother, was killed while serving as marshal of Dodge City.*

(Courtesy Kansas State Historical Society)

street carrying shotguns. The fight stopped. Bat paid a small fine. Then the Masterson brothers left Dodge on the evening train.

Bat finally settled in Denver, and he married in 1891. He became involved in horse races and boxing matches and wrote about these sporting events for newspapers. In 1902 he accepted a job as a sportswriter for the *New York Morning Telegraph*.

The famous Western gunfighter spent the last two decades of his life in New York City. He enjoyed the bright lights of Broadway. Bat continued to be a popular sportswriter until he died, apparently from a heart attack, at his desk in 1921.

Dallas Stoudenmire, wearing his marshal's badge on the lapel of his coat.
(Author's collection)

Dallas Stoudenmire
SOLDIER, RANGER, AND MARSHAL

Dallas Stoudenmire was a violent man in a violent land. Big and strong, he never backed away from a fight. Fortunately, most of his fights were on the side of law and order.

Dallas was born and raised in Alabama. When he was sixteen, in 1862, he joined the Confederate Army. For three years, Dallas fought in Civil War battles. He was wounded several times before the war ended.

After the war, Dallas moved to Texas. He farmed for a few years, then joined the Texas Rangers. With the Rangers, he rode against Comanche war parties.

Dallas served with the Texas Rangers for two years. After leaving the Rangers, he had trouble with a man who wanted to shoot him. One day in 1876, Dallas saw this man while he was riding. They stepped off their horses and began shooting at each other. After several shots apiece, Dallas killed his opponent.

The next year, Dallas was at a big party when a fight broke out, and men began firing their guns. Dallas wounded several men. Then he was wounded and tied up. Later that night, when his guard went to sleep, Dallas slipped out of his ropes and escaped.

In 1878 Dallas and some of his friends approached another group of men led by the Sparks brothers. Both groups claimed the same herd of cattle. Angrily, all of the men went for their guns. The fight ended when one of the Sparks brothers was badly wounded and two of his friends were killed.

By now, Dallas had a reputation as a brave and dangerous gunfighter. He always wore two revolvers.

In 1881 he was hired to be city marshal of El Paso. In that wild Texas border town, there was tension between Texans and Mexicans. Fights often broke out. El Paso needed a city marshal who could enforce the law.

On April 14, 1881, just four days after Dallas pinned on his badge, a bloody shootout exploded in El Paso. While Dallas was eating lunch, Constable Gus Kremkau was shot in the street. John Hale and George Campbell thought that Gus was on the side of the Mexicans. The three men argued, then Gus was shot by Hale.

Dallas pulled his revolvers and ran into the street. He began shooting at Hale. A bystander was hit, and died the next day. Hale ducked for cover. But when Hale stuck his head out for a look, Dallas killed him with a bullet in the brain.

Although dying, Gus wounded George Campbell in the wrist and foot. Then Dallas finished Campbell with a bullet in the stomach.

Three nights later, enemies of the law set an ambush for the deadly new marshal. Dallas and his brother-in-law, Doc Cummings, walked into the trap. A bushwhacker named Bill Johnson suddenly fired a shotgun. Dallas and Doc instantly drew their pistols and opened fire. Bill Johnson was killed by eight bullets.

Other hidden bushwhackers then began shooting. Dallas was hit in the foot, but he charged the bushwhackers' position. They fled into the darkness.

On the night of December 16, 1881, another El Paso thug set an ambush for Marshal Stoudenmire. The bullets missed, but the gun flashes temporarily blinded Dallas. The brave marshal drew his guns and began firing, and the bushwhackers ran away.

"I don't believe the bullet was ever molded that will kill me," said Dallas. But he was wrong.

A lawman like Dallas made many enemies. Even after Dallas left his marshal's job, he continued to feud with the three Manning brothers—Jim, Doc, and Frank. On September 18, 1882, Dallas and Doc Manning met at an El Paso saloon. Doc drew a revolver and shot Dallas in the arm and chest. Dallas pulled his gun and shot Doc in the arm. Doc dropped his gun, but began to wrestle with Dallas.

Frank Manning heard the shooting and ran to his brother's rescue. While Doc and Dallas fought, Frank put his gun against Dallas's head and pulled the trigger. Dallas dropped dead.

Dallas Stoudenmire had been a soldier, a Texas Ranger, and marshal of one of the toughest towns in the West. But he was only thirty-six years old when the Manning brothers shot him to death.

Heck Thomas was a fearless and dedicated Western lawman.
(Courtesy Western Historical Collections,
University of Oklahoma Library)

Heck Thomas
ONE OF THE THREE GUARDSMEN

All of his life, Heck Thomas answered the call of duty. He was only a boy during the Civil War, but he wanted to help defend his Georgia home. Too young to be a soldier, he ran away and carried messages for Gen. Stonewall Jackson instead.

In 1871, when Heck was twenty-one, he married a preacher's daughter from Atlanta, Georgia. Heck and his wife began to have children. Within a few years, Heck moved his growing family to Texas, where he worked as a railroad guard.

In 1878, near Dallas, the Sam Bass gang robbed a train Heck was guarding. The outlaws shot the express car full of holes, and Heck was wounded in the neck. Heck could not shoot back, because the outlaws used innocent men as shields.

The outlaws began chopping through the door to the express car. Heck hid money packages containing $22,000. When the outlaws found some packages, they happily rode away. Later they found only $89 in the fake packages.

In 1885 Heck was hired by the Fort Worth Detective Association. Heck and Deputy U.S. Marshal Jim Taylor began searching for murderers Pink and Jim Lee. There was a large reward for the two brothers.

After two months, the lawmen found the Lee brothers. From a distance of seventy-five yards, Heck and Jim shouted for the outlaws to surrender. Instead, the Lees went for their guns. The lawmen immediately killed Pink. Jim Lee fired three shots before he was hit in the throat and died.

Soon Heck was made a deputy U.S. marshal. He moved his family to Fort Smith, Arkansas. The court at Fort Smith was run by the famous "hanging judge," Isaac Parker.

Heck hunted outlaws in lawless Indian Territory (present-day Oklahoma). The work was dangerous. During his first two years, fifteen lawmen were killed in Indian Territory. Once, when Heck took his wife for a buggy ride, an outlaw tried to steal their horses. Heck wounded the man, then handcuffed him and took him to Fort Smith in the buggy. Heck's wife could not stand such a dangerous life. She took their children back to Georgia and divorced Heck.

In 1888 Heck led a posse after a gang of train robbers. When the lawmen closed in, Heck ordered the outlaws to surrender. But the outlaw leader shot Heck twice. The posse members gunned down the outlaw leader, and the rest of the gang surrendered.

While Heck recovered from his wounds, he met a schoolteacher named Mattie Mowbray. Like his first wife, Mattie was a preacher's daughter. Heck and Mattie fell in love. After they married, Heck began raising a second family.

While chasing a killer named Ned Christie, Heck shot the outlaw in the face. Ned escaped, but he was blinded in one eye and his nose was shattered. In another incident, in 1890, Heck had to kill a thief named Jim July.

In 1893, Heck was assigned to help the famous lawman Bill Tilghman in trying to tame Perry, an Oklahoma boomtown of 25,000. There were 100 saloons in Perry. During the next three years, Heck arrested more than 300 lawbreakers.

By 1896 Heck was on the trail of Bill Doolin, leader of a gang called the "Oklahombres." One night Heck and a posse trapped Doolin. Bill tried to shoot his way past the posse, but Heck and another posse member killed Doolin with shotgun blasts.

Early in the 1900s, Heck served as police chief of Lawton, Oklahoma. But his health began to fail. He died in Lawton at the age of sixty-two.

By the time of his death, Heck was famous as one of the "Three Guardsmen." This trio of noted Oklahoma lawmen was Bill Tilghman, Chris Madsen, and Heck Thomas.

Texas Ranger Captain John Hughes in retirement, shown in 1938 leading a parade in El Paso. (Author's collection)

John Hughes
THE BORDER BOSS

The Texas Ranger captain who became famous as "The Border Boss" never intended to become a lawman. John Hughes left his Illinois home to become a cowboy. He arrived in Texas at the age of fourteen. Like other Texans, he began wearing a revolver.

When John was fifteen, a man attacked his boss. John tried to defend his boss, but John was shot in the right arm. Although his arm was crippled, he practiced shooting with his left hand. John became so good with a gun that everyone thought he was a natural lefthander.

John spent the next few years as a cowboy. He helped drive several herds from Texas to the Kansas cattle towns. In 1878 he started a small horse ranch north of Austin. For years he worked horses on his ranch.

In 1886 six rustlers stole nearly 100 horses from ranches north of Austin. Eighteen of the stolen horses belonged to John. He rode after the rustlers with forty-three dollars in his pocket. John chased them for almost a year. He rode 1,200 miles and spent all but seventy-six cents of his money. During the chase, John used up nine horses. One of the horses was killed during a shootout with the rustlers. Twice the rustlers set ambushes, but John shot his way to safety both times.

Finally, John caught up with the outlaws. A sheriff and a deputy sheriff were with him. A shootout began, and four of the outlaws were killed. The other outlaws surrendered. At last, John drove the stolen horses back to their home ranches.

The year-long chase made John a famous manhunter. Friends of the outlaws twice tried to bushwhack John. Once he was wounded, but both times he fired back and drove the bushwhackers away.

Texas Ranger Ira Aten asked John to help him chase a murderer named Judd Roberts. For a month Aten and John tracked the outlaw. At last they found him at the home of his sweetheart in the Texas Panhandle. Roberts tried to shoot his way to freedom. But when Aten and John opened fire, Roberts was hit with six bullets. He confessed his crimes before he died in the arms of his sweetheart.

Ira Aten persuaded John to join the Texas Rangers. John was assigned to Company D of the famous Frontier Battalion of Texas Rangers. Company D tried to protect the border country along the Rio Grande in southwest Texas. John soon was promoted to corporal.

In 1889 ore robberies had occurred at the gold mines of Shafter, Texas. John began working as a gold miner to trap the outlaws. He found out that a mine foreman was telling the thieves when an ore shipment was scheduled.

John and two other Rangers finally caught the thieves transporting stolen ore into Mexico. The criminals resisted arrest with rifle fire. The shootout lasted for an hour, and the Rangers killed three of the four thieves. The other robber surrendered. The next day John arrested the crooked mine foreman.

On Christmas Day in 1889, John set an ambush for cattle rustlers Will and Alvin Odle. With John were Ira Aten and two other lawmen. The Odle brothers were hiding in Mexico. On Christmas night they tried to sneak across the border. John saw them riding in the moonlight and ordered them to surrender. When the brothers tried to fight, the lawmen opened fire. The outlaws were shot off their horses and died within minutes.

In 1893 John and Ranger Lon Oden were chasing three Mexican outlaws along the Rio Grande. One of the outlaws shot Oden's horse, but John and Oden killed the outlaw.

Also in 1893, Capt. Frank Jones was killed in a fight with outlaws

on the border. Jones was the captain of Company D. By this time John had been promoted to sergeant. Now he was promoted to captain. As captain of Company D, John became known as "The Border Boss."

In 1896 Capt. John Hughes and three members of Company D chased a bandit leader named Miguel de la Torre. The Rangers found the bandit in Lajitas, a village on the Rio Grande. John rode up to the bandit, dismounted, and wrestled with him. Within moments the bandit had been placed on a horse and handcuffed to the saddle.

The bandit's friends started shooting at the Rangers. Hughes and his men stood behind their horses and fired back. The Rangers wounded three men, then rode out of town with their prisoner.

Later in 1896, John led a posse after three horse rustlers. The outlaws fired their rifles at the posse, but John led a charge. One outlaw was killed and another escaped. The third rustler was wounded, but he fired his pistol at John and Ranger Thalis Cook. John and Cook fired one more shot apiece, and the outlaw fell dead.

For two more decades John continued to protect the border with Company D. He retired in 1915, after twenty-eight years as a Texas Ranger, but remained in El Paso, where Company D had headquartered.

John was very religious. He did not drink or smoke. He lived to be ninety-two. When asked why he never married, John had this to say: "An officer who hunts desperate criminals has no business having a wife and family, and I have remained single."

The Border Boss also spoke about his gunfights with outlaws. "I have never lost a battle," said John, "and never let a prisoner escape."

Harry Wheeler was captain of the Arizona Rangers and sheriff of Cochise County at Tombstone, Arizona.

(Courtesy Arizona Historical Society)

Harry Wheeler
THE GREATEST ARIZONA RANGER

Harry Wheeler was a U.S. cavalryman, a sheriff, an army captain during World War I, and a mounted inspector along the Arizona-Mexico border. But Harry's finest work was as an Arizona Ranger.

Harry enlisted as a private in the Arizona Rangers. Soon he was promoted to sergeant, then lieutenant, then captain. He was the only man to hold every rank as an Arizona Ranger. Harry Wheeler became the best officer who ever served with the Rangers.

Harry's father was an army officer, so Harry grew up in Western forts. He was taught to shoot, and became an expert with a pistol and rifle.

In 1897 Harry enlisted in the U.S. Cavalry at Fort Sill, Oklahoma. The next year he married Mamie Stafford. Harry and Mamie became the parents of a son and a daughter.

Harry was transferred to Fort Grant, Arizona. When he left the army in 1901, Harry decided to make his home in Arizona.

The Arizona Rangers were organized in 1901. There were so many robberies and shootings that the U.S. Congress would not admit the Arizona Territory as a state. So the Arizona Legislature organized a ranger company to stop the outlaws. If the Arizona Rangers could establish law and order, Arizona could become a state.

Harry Wheeler enlisted in the Rangers in 1903. He impressed everyone with his courage and sense of duty. Within four months, he was promoted to sergeant.

On October 22, 1904, Sergeant Wheeler broke up a robbery at a saloon in Tucson. "Don't go in there," he was warned, "there is a holdup going on!"

"All right," replied Harry, "that's what I'm here for."

Harry drew his six-gun and entered the saloon. The masked bandit, Joe Bostwick, turned to shoot at the lawman. But Harry fired first. The bullet grazed Bostwick in the forehead. Bostwick triggered a wild shot before Harry shot him in the chest. The bandit groaned and dropped to the floor.

Bostwick died two nights later. "I am sorry that this happened," said Harry, "but it was either his life or mine . . ."

A few months later, Harry was promoted to lieutenant. Now he was second-in-command of the Rangers to Capt. Tom Rynning.

In February 1907 Lieutenant Wheeler and Captain Rynning were in Benson, Arizona. On the morning of February 28, Harry learned that a man carrying a gun had just arrived on a train. The man was J. A. Tracy, and he was looking for another man who had stolen his girlfriend.

Harry hurried to the train station. He hoped to stop the trouble before there was any shooting. J. A. Tracy stepped off the railroad car.

"Hold on there," ordered Harry. "I arrest you. Give me that gun."

Instead, Tracy fired a bullet that tore a hole in Harry's coat. Harry quickly drew his gun and opened fire. He shot Tracy four times—under the heart, and in the neck, arm, and leg. Tracy shot Harry in the upper leg, then fell down.

"I am all in," gasped Tracy. "My gun is empty."

Harry limped toward the fallen man. But Tracy had two bullets left. He fired again, hitting Harry in the foot. Harry's gun was empty, but he threw rocks at Tracy. Finally, Tracy ran out of bullets.

"Well," said Harry, "it was a great fight while it lasted, wasn't it?"

"I'll get you yet," muttered Tracy. He died, however, within a few minutes.

Later it was learned that Tracy was wanted for two murders in Nevada. Harry was given a $500 reward. But Harry did not want money for killing someone. He gave the money to the widow of one of the men Tracy had murdered.

One month after Harry killed J. A. Tracy, Captain Rynning resigned from the Rangers. Harry was promoted to captain.

He now commanded the Arizona Rangers. Harry was an excellent leader. He continued to make many arrests.

On the night of May 6, 1908, Harry set a trap for a horse thief named George Arnett. A deputy sheriff was with Harry. Late that night, Arnett rode into the trap. He tried to shoot his way to freedom, but the two lawmen opened fire and killed the outlaw.

The Rangers killed or arrested most of the outlaws in Arizona. The Arizona Legislature decided that the Rangers were no longer needed. In February 1909 the legislature abolished the Arizona Rangers.

Capt. Harry Wheeler (left) about to lead an Arizona Ranger patrol.
(Courtesy Arizona Historical Society)

Soon Harry became a deputy sheriff of Cochise County. Later he served as a mounted inspector for the U.S. Customs Service. Then, in 1911, Harry was elected sheriff of Cochise County.

Harry moved with his family to Tombstone, the county seat. He was an excellent sheriff. He often led posses chasing after outlaws, and twice he was reelected sheriff.

During World War I, Harry wanted to serve in the army. He resigned as sheriff and was made an army captain. But the war ended before he was shipped overseas to fight.

Sadly, Harry's seventeen-year-old son was killed in an accident. Harry and his wife divorced. Then Harry remarried and had three more children.

Harry served on the police force at Douglas, Arizona, before he began ranching. A superb rifle shot, Harry was a champion in shooting matches.

In 1925 Harry Wheeler died of pneumonia at the age of fifty. At his funeral, he was praised for his bravery and sense of duty in serving Arizona and his country.

Jim Roberts
THE LAST GUNFIGHTER

Jim Roberts became famous as a gunfighter during Arizona's Pleasant Valley War. This bloody range war exploded in 1887, when the Tewksbury and Graham families tried to drive each other out of Pleasant Valley.

Jim fought on the side of his friends, the Tewksburys. During one fight, Jim aimed his rifle at John Paine. Paine was hiding behind a horse, and Jim shot his ear off. Paine jumped up. When he tried to run away, Jim killed him.

More than twenty men were killed during the Pleasant Valley War. Jim was considered the best fighting man on the Tewksbury side.

Following the end of the feud, Jim became a deputy sheriff. Then he was constable and city marshal for many years in Jerome, a tough Arizona mining town. In Jerome he had to kill several lawbreakers. He last wore a badge in Clarksdale, Arizona.

In 1928, when the lawman was seventy, two thieves robbed the Bank of Arizona in Clarksdale. They jumped into their car with $50,000 of stolen money. As they drove away from the bank, Jim drew his old Colt revolver. He shot the driver of the car in the head. The car crashed into a school building. Then Jim arrested the other young bank robber.

It was the last gunfight for the last Western gunfighter. He continued to patrol the streets of Clarksdale until he suffered a heart attack and died in 1934.

Western Outlaws

Billy the Kid and Jesse James were two of the most famous men in the West. But they were famous because they broke the law. Billy the Kid murdered a sheriff and two jail guards, and he stole horses. Jesse James killed innocent people while robbing banks.

Cole Younger also was famous as a thief and killer. And almost everyone in the West was afraid of Wes Hardin and Harvey Logan. Both of these men were mean, vicious killers.

But like most outlaws, these famous Western desperadoes paid for their crimes. Billy the Kid was only twenty-one when he was killed by Sheriff Pat Garrett. Jesse James was murdered for reward money. Cole Younger was wounded eleven times by a posse, then sent to prison until he was an old man. Wes Hardin served fifteen years in prison, then was shot in the back of the head. Harvey Logan was killed after a train robbery.

Crime did not pay in the Old West.

Jesse James led one of the most famous outlaw gangs in the West.
(Author's collection)

Jesse James
A LEGENDARY OUTLAW

Jesse James was a thief and a killer. But somehow he became a legendary hero to people from his home state of Missouri.

Jesse and his older brother, Frank, were raised on a Missouri farm. During the Civil War, Jesse and Frank fought under William Quantrill and "Bloody" Bill Anderson. Quantrill and Anderson claimed to be Confederate soldiers. Actually, they were only outlaw raiders who robbed and killed.

Although Jesse was still a teenager during the war, he was wounded twice. On September 27, 1864, Anderson led Jesse and other raiders into Centralia, Missouri. In Centralia they murdered twenty-five unarmed Union soldiers. They were pursued by Maj. A. V. Johnson and a large force of Union soldiers.

"Bloody" Bill Anderson set an ambush, and Major Johnson, along with one hundred of his men, was killed. Jesse James was credited with killing Major Johnson in battle.

After the war ended, Jesse and Frank could not settle down to farm life. They formed a gang with other raiders, such as the Younger brothers—Cole, Jim, and Bob.

On February 16, 1866, the James-Younger Gang rode into Liberty, Missouri. The gang stole nearly $60,000 from the Clay County Savings Bank. The bandits killed a young college student. This was the first daylight bank robbery ever committed in the United States.

The gang continued robbing banks for years. During one robbery Jesse shot the bank president. In other robberies, bank employees were killed by members of the gang. In 1873 the James-Younger Gang also began to rob trains.

A large reward was offered for anyone who could capture Jesse and Frank. Detectives began to hide near the farm of their mother. In March 1874 a Pinkerton detective was killed near the farm. Jesse and Frank were blamed for shooting the detective.

A year later, bounty hunters came to the James farm during the night. They set fire to the house, and there was an explosion. The nine-year-old half-brother of Jesse and Frank was killed, and their mother lost a hand in the explosion.

In 1874 Jesse married his lifelong sweetheart, Zee Mimms. Jesse and Zee became the parents of a daughter and a son. Because Jesse was being hunted by lawmen, the family had to keep moving, and Jesse often changed his name.

In 1876 the James-Younger Gang tried to rob the First National Bank of Northfield, Minnesota. But bank cashier Joseph Heywood refused to open the safe. One of the robbers cut his throat, then shot him.

When the gang tried to ride out of town, citizens opened fire. The outlaws killed one of the townspeople. But the townspeople killed two other robbers, Clell Miller and William Stiles. The other six members galloped out of town.

The gang was chased by several posses. Jesse and Frank left the other four outlaws. The James brothers managed to escape, and rode home to Missouri.

Cole and Jim Younger and Charlie Pitts stayed with the wounded Bob Younger. But a posse closed in and killed Charlie Pitts. The three Younger brothers were wounded several times. The Youngers surrendered and were sent to prison.

Frank and Jesse moved their families to Tennessee for a few years. Then Jesse formed a new gang. In 1881 they robbed a train at Winston, Missouri. The leader of the gang wore a beard, but witnesses thought it was Jesse. He killed the conductor of the train and a passenger during the robbery.

Jesse went into hiding with his family. They lived in a small house in St. Joseph, Missouri. Jesse used the alias "Thomas Howard" and began to plan new robberies.

One of the gang members, Bob Ford, planned to kill Jesse for the reward money. On April 3, 1881, Ford shot Jesse in the back of the head. (In 1892, Ford was killed during a saloon fight in Colorado.)

Jesse was thirty-four when he was murdered. He was buried in the front yard of his mother's farm. She charged visitors twenty-five cents to tour the home and Jesse's grave. The farm is still open to tourists today.

Cole Younger *(left) and his brother Jim.*

(Author's collection)

Cole Younger
A ROUGH MAN WITH ROUGH WAYS

Cole Younger was a bold robber of banks and trains. He was not a cold-blooded killer, but he often used his guns while committing crimes. And his brothers joined him in robberies and shootouts.

Thomas Coleman Younger was the seventh of fourteen children. Cole was born in 1844 and raised on the family farm in Missouri.

During the Civil War, Cole fought in the Confederate Army. He also rode with the outlaw raiders of William Clarke Quantrill. Jesse and Frank James also were raiders under Quantrill.

On November 10, 1861, Cole killed for the first time during a fight with Union troops. He killed a soldier with an amazing pistol shot measured at seventy-one yards.

In 1862 Cole's father was murdered. On Christmas Day, Cole learned that the killers were in Kansas City, Missouri. Cole found one of his father's killers in a saloon. There was a fight, and Cole killed the man.

The next year Cole was on army duty in Texas. In Dallas he met a girl who later would become known as the female outlaw Belle Starr. For a time Cole and Belle were sweethearts.

After the Civil War, Cole returned to Missouri. There he met two farmers, Jesse and Frank James. Jesse, Frank, and Cole had ridden with Quantrill during the war. Soon they formed a gang and robbed a bank.

The James-Younger Gang committed many other bank robberies. But Cole did not like Jesse James very much. Cole led several robberies himself, and his younger brothers, Jim and Bob, helped.

In 1872 Cole led four other men in robbing the Deposit Bank of Columbia, Kentucky. The bank's cashier, R.A.C. Martin, went for a gun. But the outlaw leader shot Martin in the head.

The last robbery of the James-Younger Gang was a disaster. In 1876 eight members of the gang tried to rob the First National Bank of Northfield, Minnesota. The outlaws killed the bank cashier, Joseph Heywood. Citizens began to shoot at the gang as they made their escape. Clell Miller and William Stiles were killed. Bob Younger was badly wounded and his horse was killed.

But Cole picked up his brother and put him behind his saddle. The outlaws shot their way out of town, killing one of the townspeople.

Several posses gave chase. Frank and Jesse James rode off toward Missouri by themselves, but Bob Younger was hurt too badly to escape. Cole and Jim Younger stayed with their wounded brother, and so did Charlie Pitts. These four outlaws tried to hide from the posses, but there were several fights. After two weeks, a six-man posse found the outlaws hiding in a swamp. A vicious fight broke out.

Three of the lawmen were wounded, and Charlie Pitts was killed. Cole Younger had been wounded eleven times, Jim Younger had been shot five times, and Bob four times. The Younger brothers surrendered.

Cole, Jim, and Bob were thrown into a wagon and taken to the nearest town. Despite his eleven wounds, Cole stood up in the wagon and bowed to the ladies. Bob told a newspaper reporter: "We are rough men and used to rough ways."

After recovering, the brothers were sent to prison. Bob caught tuberculosis and died in 1889. Jim and Cole were released from prison in 1901. But Jim's health failed, and he committed suicide the next year.

Cole teamed up with Frank James to appear at Wild West shows. Cole also lectured about his adventures and the evils of crime. Finally, he retired to the old family home in Missouri.

Cole Younger died in 1916 at the age of seventy-two. He was buried beside Jim and Bob and their mother.

Billy the Kid
MOST FAMOUS OUTLAW

Billy the Kid was the most famous outlaw gunfighter in the Old West.

Born in 1859, probably in New York City, his real name was Henry McCarty. After he became an outlaw he had several aliases, including "William Bonney." But most people called him "Billy the Kid."

When he was a boy his family moved west, finally settling in New Mexico. But by the time he was thirteen, both his father and mother had died.

Billy became a cowboy. He worked in Arizona, but soon he was in trouble for stealing. Then, when he was seventeen, he had a fight with a blacksmith. The big man threw Billy to the floor. Billy drew a six-gun and shot the blacksmith, who died the next day. Billy was put in jail, but he escaped and returned to New Mexico.

In New Mexico he was hired as a cowboy by Lincoln County rancher John Tunstall. Soon afterward, Tunstall was murdered by a large group of his enemies. The death of John Tunstall triggered a bloody range war, which became known as the Lincoln County War.

Billy the Kid vowed to kill the men who had murdered his boss. The Kid joined a gang of "Regulators" who wanted revenge. The Regulators were led by Dick Brewer, who had been John Tunstall's foreman.

In March 1878 Brewer and the Regulators chased down William Morton and Frank Baker. Morton and Baker were two of the main

From the age of seventeen to twenty-one, Billy the Kid was involved in sixteen gunfights.

(Author's collection)

suspects in the murder of Tunstall. Morton killed one of the Regulators. But Billy the Kid and the other Regulators killed Morton and Baker.

The Regulators blamed Sheriff William Brady for the death of John Tunstall. On April 1, 1878, Billy the Kid led four other Regulators into the town of Lincoln to find Sheriff Brady. The Regulators hid behind a low wall and waited.

Soon Sheriff Brady and four deputies walked up the street near the wall. Billy the Kid and his men jumped up and opened fire. Sheriff Brady and Deputy George Hindman were killed. Another deputy was wounded. Billy the Kid received a slight wound. The Regulators ran for their horses and rode out of town.

Three days later, a large group of Regulators stopped at Blazer's Mill to eat lunch. While they were eating, one of their enemies, "Buckshot" Roberts, rode up to the mill. Shooting broke out between Roberts and the Regulators. Roberts wounded two of the Regulators, and he shot the hat off Billy the Kid's head. Billy's pal, Charlie Bowdre, shot Roberts in the stomach.

Everyone took cover. Even though Roberts was dying, he continued to fight. When Dick Brewer raised his head to look for Roberts, Buckshot killed him with a rifle shot. The Regulators rode off with their wounded. Roberts soon died, and the Battle of Blazer's Mill ended.

During the next few months, Billy the Kid was involved in several little fights with enemies of the Regulators. In July 1878 the two sides battled for five days in Lincoln.

During the Battle of Lincoln, Billy and several other Regulators defended a large adobe house. The house was set on fire. As the house burned slowly, the Regulators retreated from room to room. After dark, the Regulators tried to shoot their way to safety. Men were shot on both sides, but Billy was not hit, and he escaped into the darkness. The Regulators had been defeated at the Battle of Lincoln.

Billy the Kid then formed a gang of rustlers. Although he was an outlaw, he had hideouts in Lincoln County. And he had many friends and sweethearts among the Mexican population.

One of his favorite hangouts was at Fort Sumner. On the night of January 10, 1880, Billy was having a good time in a Fort Sumner saloon.

A man named Joe Grant was there, and he wanted to kill the famous Billy the Kid. Grant pulled a gun on Billy, but the Kid shot him in the mouth.

That year Pat Garrett was elected sheriff. His main job was to halt the outlawry in Lincoln County. The tall Sheriff Garrett began to hunt Billy the Kid and his gang.

On the night of December 19, 1880, the Kid and five of his men rode into Fort Sumner to have some fun. But Sheriff Garrett and a posse were waiting. The lawman opened fire, and Tom O'Folliard was shot in the chest. O'Folliard was captured by the posse and soon died, while Billy the Kid and the other outlaws galloped away into the night.

Billy and his men hid out in an old rock cabin. Within four days, however, Pat Garrett found the cabin. Charlie Bowdre was killed by the lawmen. The cabin was surrounded, and the outlaws realized they could not escape. Billy the Kid and his friends surrendered.

At his trial, Billy the Kid was convicted of murder. He was sentenced to be hanged in Lincoln on May 13, 1881. Two weeks before the hanging, though, the Kid escaped from jail.

Someone had smuggled a gun to Billy, probably in the outhouse behind the jail. When the guard took Billy back upstairs to his cell, the Kid pulled his gun. The guard, J. W. Bell, tried to run away, but the Kid fired. Bell died within minutes.

Another guard, Bob Olinger, had taken the other prisoners across the street to eat supper. Olinger heard the gunfire and ran toward the jail.

"Hello, Bob," said the Kid from an upstairs window. He had picked up a double-barreled shotgun.

Olinger looked up just as the Kid fired both barrels of the shotgun. Olinger was killed by the blast of thirty-six buckshot.

No one tried to stop the Kid as he rode out of town. For the next three months, he hid with his friends while Sheriff Pat Garrett hunted for him.

Garrett suspected that the Kid would try to visit his sweetheart in Fort Sumner. The sheriff guessed right. On the night of July 14, 1881, Garrett slipped into the dark bedroom of Pete Maxwell, who knew Billy. The sheriff sat on the side of Maxwell's bed and asked if Pete had seen

The two-story courthouse and jail in Lincoln, where Billy the Kid escaped by killing two guards. The upstairs window on the right is where the Kid shotgunned Bob Olinger.

(Author's collection)

the Kid. Suddenly, the Kid appeared in the doorway. He had spent the evening in Fort Sumner with his sweetheart. Now he was hungry. The Kid was holding a butcher knife. He had come to ask Maxwell if he could cut a steak from a side of beef in the meat house.

When he noticed someone sitting on the side of the bed, he asked, "¿Quién es?" ("Who is it?").

Sheriff Pat Garrett quickly fired his gun. The bullet struck the young outlaw in the heart. He fell dead on his back. The next day, Billy the Kid was buried in the Fort Sumner cemetery between two of his outlaw pals, Tom O'Folliard and Charlie Bowdre.

Billy the Kid died at the age of twenty-one. During the last four years of his life, the Kid fought in sixteen gunfights. He killed four men and helped to kill five others. Although many people liked him, he could not stay out of trouble. Billy the Kid was an outlaw and a killer.

Wes Hardin was a vicious, cold-blooded killer.

(Author's collection)

Wes Hardin
DEADLY SON OF A PREACHER

John Wesley Hardin was born in Texas in 1853. He was the son of a Methodist preacher. His father hoped the boy would become a preacher. He was named after John Wesley, who had founded the Methodist religion. But Wes would become one of the meanest killers in the West.

At the age of eleven Wes had a fight with another boy. Wes pulled a knife and stabbed the boy in the chest and back. The boy lived, but Wes had revealed his violent temper.

Like most Texas boys, Wes learned to shoot early in his life. He loved guns. He practiced until he became an expert shot. Wes liked to carry two guns, often in shoulder holsters. And he never hesitated to use his guns.

When he was fifteen, in 1868, Wes had trouble with a man named Mage. Mage threatened Wes with a stick, so Wes pulled a revolver and fired three slugs into the man's chest. Mage died a few days later.

During the next few years, Wes was chased by lawmen and soldiers. Sometimes he shot these pursuers from ambush. He was arrested once, but while he was being taken to Waco for trial he managed to obtain a gun. Wes killed a guard and escaped.

Wes liked to gamble, and often he quarreled with other players over a card game. In 1869 a gambler named Bradly took a shot at him. Wes shot Bradly in the head and chest. There would be other killings over card games.

In 1871 Wes left Texas to go on a cattle drive to Kansas. But in Abilene, Kansas, he killed a man named Charles Cougar. The next day he killed a man named Juan Bideno.

Back in Texas, in 1873, he killed Deputy Sheriff J. B. Morgan, in Cuero. A few months later Wes killed Sheriff Jack Helm. The next year, in Comanche, Texas, he shot Deputy Sheriff Charles Webb in the head. Wes was wounded, but managed to escape.

In 1872, when he was eighteen, Wes married Jane Bowen. The couple eventually had a son and two daughters. After the killing of Charles Webb, a $4,000 reward was posted for Wes. He decided to change his name, and he took his family to Florida.

Texas Ranger John Armstrong found Wes in Florida in 1877. Armstrong arrested Wes on a train and had to shoot a man sitting beside Wes. The outlaw had gone for his gun, but the weapon caught in his suspenders. Armstrong hit Wes over the head with his gun barrel.

The Ranger took Wes back to Texas, where the outlaw was sentenced to a long prison term. His wife died while he was in prison. During the fifteen years Wes spent behind bars, he studied to become a lawyer.

When he left prison in 1894, however, Wes continued to get into trouble. Now in his forties, he married a teenaged girl. He drank and gambled. Wes moved to El Paso, a tough town where he made many enemies.

Wes threatened to kill two law officers, John Selman and his son, John Selman, Jr. Old John Selman was an experienced gunfighter who realized how dangerous Wes Hardin was.

On the night of August 19, 1895, Wes was playing dice in the Acme Saloon in El Paso. Old John Selman walked into the saloon and shot Wes in the back of the head. As Wes fell to the floor, Selman fired three more times. (The next year, Selman was killed in another El Paso gunfight.)

Before he died, Wes wrote a book about his life. He bragged that he had killed more than forty men. Although he did not kill forty men, he probably killed about half that many. John Wesley Hardin, a Methodist preacher's son, killed more men than any other gunfighter.

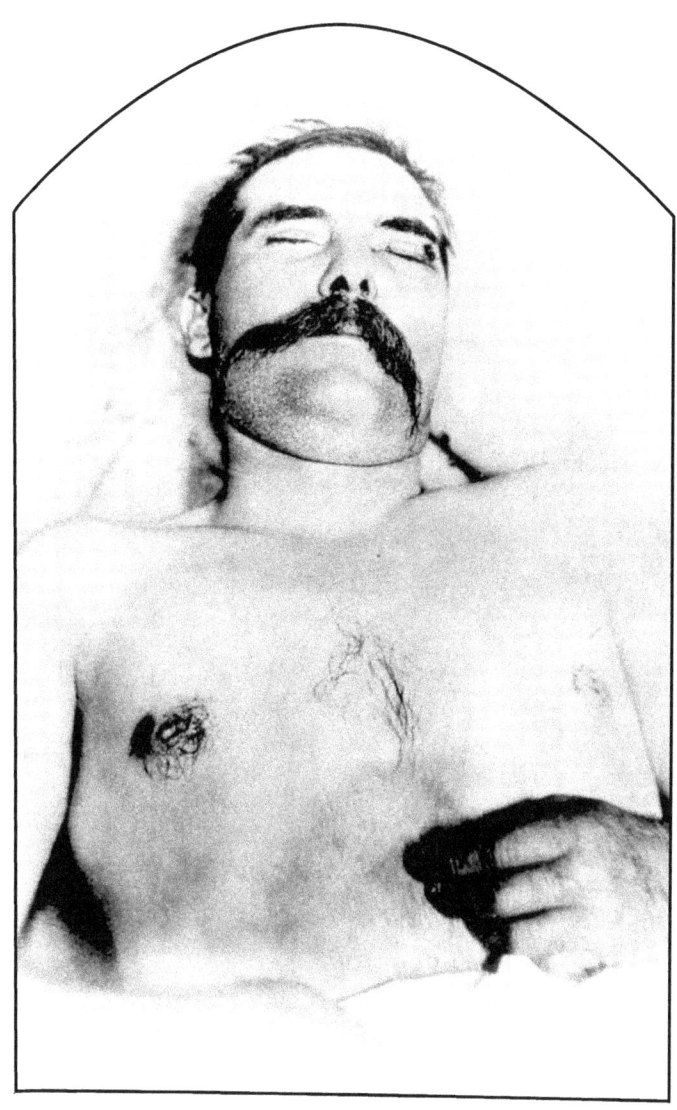

Wes Hardin, after being shot to death by John Selman.
(Courtesy Western History Collections,
University of Oklahoma Library)

![Photograph of the Wild Bunch]

The Wild Bunch on vacation in Fort Worth in 1900 after a robbery. Harvey Logan, the "Tiger of the Wild Bunch," stands at right. Standing at left is Will Carver. Seated left to right: The Sundance Kid, Ben Kilpatrick, and Butch Cassidy.

(Courtesy Western History Collections,
University of Oklahoma Library)

Harvey Logan
THE TIGER OF THE WILD BUNCH

One of the most famous outlaw gangs of the Old West was the Wild Bunch. The Wild Bunch was led by Butch Cassidy and the Sundance Kid. But Butch and Sundance never killed anyone during their robberies. That job was left to the most dangerous member of the Wild Bunch, Harvey Logan. Harvey was called the "Tiger of the Wild Bunch."

Harvey was born in 1865. He and his three younger brothers were orphaned when they were children. The Logan boys were raised by an aunt in Missouri.

When Harvey was nineteen, he left home to travel to the West. Two of his teenaged brothers, Lonie and Johnny, and a cousin, Bob Lee, went with him.

The boys wandered to Wyoming, where they became rustlers. In 1888 they used a stolen herd of cattle to start a ranch near Landusky, Montana. Harvey soon became a heavy drinker. When he drank, he had a mean temper.

Harvey drank heavily in Landusky on Christmas Eve of 1894. With him were his brother Lonie and another rustler, Jim Thornhill. The three rustlers began to fire their guns. Finally, they were confronted by Pike Landusky, the founder of the little town.

Harvey and Pike began to fight. Lonie Logan and Jim Thornhill drew their pistols and held the crowd back. Pike was more than thirty years older than Harvey. Harvey soon whipped the older man. Then Harvey began to pound the older man's head against the floor. Finally, Pike drew a gun—but Harvey quickly pulled his own gun and shot Pike to death.

In January 1896 the Logan brothers had trouble with Montana rancher Jim Winters. Winters aimed his rifle and killed Johnny Logan. Harvey and Lonie opened fire, but Winters continued to shoot, and the brothers were driven away. Five years later, Harvey returned and killed Winters.

By the late 1890s Harvey and Lonie had joined the Wild Bunch. Between robberies, the gang hid out in the rugged Hole-in-the-Wall country of Wyoming.

Following a bank robbery in 1897, a posse chased Harvey and two other gang members. After a shootout, the outlaws were captured. They were jailed in Deadwood, South Dakota, but Harvey and his two companions soon escaped.

In 1899 the Wild Bunch pulled a train robbery at Wilcox, Wyoming. The gang scattered after the robbery. Harvey made camp with the Sundance Kid and "Flat Nose" Curry. While they were eating supper, they were attacked by a posse.

The leader of the posse was Sheriff Joe Hazen. Harvey aimed his rifle and shot Sheriff Hazen in the stomach. The three outlaws escaped on foot. Sheriff Hazen died a few hours later.

The next year Logan and a few other outlaws were being chased in Arizona by two lawmen. Harvey opened fire with his rifle. A bullet ripped through the leg of lawman George Scarborough. The bullet also killed Scarborough's horse. The outlaws escaped, and Scarborough died the next day.

Harvey next went to Utah, but within a few weeks he was trapped by a posse. Harvey drew his six-gun and shot Sheriff Jesse Tyler and Deputy Sam Jenkins. Both lawmen died, and Harvey again escaped.

A few weeks later Harvey killed two brothers. Also in 1900, Lonie Logan was killed by a posse.

Harvey now was constantly on the run from the law. In March 1901 he passed through Paint Rock, Texas. There he quarreled with a local citizen named Oliver Thornton. Harvey shot Thornton dead, then galloped out of town.

Later in 1901, Harvey tried to duck the law by heading east. But in Knoxville, Tennessee, when he had a fight with policemen, Harvey was arrested. Soon he escaped jail, using a guard as a shield, and rode away on the sheriff's horse.

Harvey returned to familiar hideouts in the West. His cohorts Butch Cassidy and the Sundance Kid had left for South America. Harvey thought about joining them. Instead, in July 1903 Harvey and two other outlaws robbed a train near Parachute, Colorado.

Soon a large posse closed in on the outlaws. A fight broke out. Harvey was badly wounded. Knowing he could not escape, Harvey shot himself in the head. The Tiger of the Wild Bunch was dead.

Henry Brown

John Selman

Tom Horn

Jim Miller

Outlaw-Lawmen

Everyone has to choose between right and wrong, between good and evil. Many Westerners stood up for what was right. Westerners who went bad became outlaws.

But some men were torn between good and evil. Sometimes they wore badges, using their guns on the side of the law, then turned bad. Other times they were outlaws who later became lawmen.

John Selman was a Texas outlaw who later became a lawman. Although Jim Miller was a murderer, sometimes he used his guns as a lawman. Tom Horn served as an army scout, a soldier, and a Pinkerton detective. But then he became a hired killer. Henry Brown was an outlaw with Billy the Kid. Then he decided to become a lawman. After Marshal Henry Brown married, he turned back to outlawry. He was killed after robbing a bank.

The decision to do the right thing turned the lives of some outlaws around. But others let their guns take control, and fell out of favor with the law.

John Selman was an outlaw who later became a lawman in El Paso. John killed Wes Hardin in 1896.

(Courtesy Western History Collections, University of Oklahoma Library)

John Selman
ON BOTH SIDES OF THE LAW

John Selman moved with his family from Arkansas to Texas in 1858, when John was eighteen years old. His father soon died, and as the oldest son, John became responsible for his mother and four younger brothers and sisters.

When the Civil War began, John joined the Confederate Cavalry. He served for two years. In 1863 he left the cavalry to move his family to a ranch on the Texas frontier. Two years later, John married. He and his wife had five children before she died in 1878.

During the 1870s, the wild town of Fort Griffin sprang up near the Selman ranch. In Fort Griffin, John met such famous gunfighters as Doc Holliday, Wyatt Earp, Bat Masterson, "Killin' Jim" Miller, and Pat Garrett. He also became friends with Sheriff John Larn. Often Selman helped the sheriff make arrests. In 1876, while helping Sheriff Larn, he killed a fugitive named Hampton. He also killed a bully named Haulph.

Unfortunately, Sheriff Larn drifted from law and order and began to steal horses and cattle. Again, he was helped by John Selman. A farmer became angry that his cattle were stolen. He fired a shotgun at John Selman. The shotgun blast tore off John's saddle horn. John opened fire and killed the farmer.

In 1878 a mob lynched the sheriff. John Selman and his brother, Tom Cat, fled to New Mexico. John joined a band of thieves led by an outlaw named Hart, but John later shot Hart in the head. John then took command of the gang, which became known as "Selman's Scouts."

Selman's Scouts robbed stores and stole cattle. Once, when John killed a member of his gang, the U.S. Cavalry rode against the gang. John and Tom Cat headed back to Texas.

By 1880, John had married again. He and his brother continued rustling in West Texas, but Tom Cat was captured and lynched. John was arrested, but he bribed his jailers and escaped.

Fleeing to Mexico, he opened a saloon, and his family joined him in Chihuahua. Years later, in 1888, John moved to El Paso, Texas.

El Paso was one of the toughest towns in the West. During a fight, John was stabbed in the face. He led cattle drives and worked at other honest jobs. The people of El Paso decided that the old gunfighter could protect them. And so, in 1892, John was elected city constable.

John became a respected lawman. In 1894 another lawman, Baz Outlaw, became drunk in El Paso. Texas Ranger Joe McKidrict tried to quiet the drunken Outlaw, but Baz angrily shot McKidrict in the head.

John Selman heard the shooting and ran to stop the trouble. Outlaw tried to shoot John in the head, but missed. John shot Outlaw in the chest. Then Outlaw shot John twice in the right leg. Baz Outlaw staggered away and died.

Although John's leg healed, he had to use a walking cane. He was proud when his son, John Selman, Jr., became a member of the El Paso police force. Both Selmans began to have trouble with John Wesley Hardin. The vicious killer threatened to kill John, Jr. Old John knew that Wes Hardin was a very dangerous man. John decided to kill Wes before he could kill one of the Selmans.

On the night of August 19, 1895, Wes Hardin was in the Acme Saloon. Suddenly, old John Selman came through the door and began shooting. A bullet hit Wes in the head. He fell to the floor as John missed with another shot. Then John walked over and shot Wes twice more.

John Selman, Jr., ran into the saloon. He grabbed his father by the arm and shouted, "Don't shoot anymore, he's dead."

Old John surrendered to his son. Everyone was glad that the vicious Wes Hardin was dead. Old John was later acquitted by a jury.

But John had trouble with lawman George Scarborough. On April 5, 1896, John and Scarborough went into an alley to talk. Then Scarborough drew his gun and shot John four times. A crowd hurried to the scene.

"Boys, you know I am not afraid of any man," gasped John, "but I never drew my gun."

The next day doctors operated, but the old gunfighter died. He was fifty-six. Using his guns on both sides of the law, John Selman had killed six men.

Henry Brown wearing his marshal's badge in Caldwell, Kansas. Before he was a lawman he was an outlaw with Billy the Kid. And while he was marshal of Caldwell, he robbed a bank in another town.

(Courtesy Kansas State Historical Society)

Henry Brown
THE OUTLAW MARSHAL

Henry Brown wore two guns. He hired his guns to both sides of New Mexico's Lincoln County War. Henry rustled horses with Billy the Kid in Lincoln County. Then he became a lawman in two of the toughest towns in the West. As he became a famous lawman, Henry got married. But then the two-gun lawman turned outlaw again.

Henry's parents died when he was a little boy. He grew up on his uncle's farm in Missouri. In 1875, when he was seventeen, Henry went west to become a cowboy.

A year later he was in a cattle camp in the Texas Panhandle. Henry always had a hot temper, and he began to fight another cowboy. Henry drew a gun and shot the cowboy three times. The wounded man died, and Henry rode out of Texas into lawless Lincoln County, New Mexico.

In 1878 Lincoln County exploded in a bloody range war. Henry Brown was a hired gunman for one of the warring sides. But he became angry when he was not paid fairly. Henry switched to the other side, the "Regulators," and became friends with a Regulator named Billy the Kid.

Henry helped Billy ambush and kill Sheriff William Brady. He fought in the Battle of Blazer's Mill a few days later. Henry also fought for five days in the Battle of Lincoln in July 1878.

The Regulators were defeated. But Billy the Kid, Henry Brown, and a few other outlaws began to steal horses. The gang drove a herd of stolen horses to Tascosa, Texas.

The horses were sold, and Billy the Kid returned to New Mexico. But Henry Brown did not want to return to New Mexico, where he was an outlaw. He decided to stay in Texas and try to live as an honest man.

Henry worked as a cowboy on a ranch near Tascosa. Then ranchers hired him to search for rustlers. (Since Henry had been a rustler, the ranchers thought he could catch other rustlers.)

Next Henry became a deputy sheriff, working out of Tascosa. Called the "Cowboy Capital of the Panhandle," Tascosa was a rough town with many gunfighters. But Henry Brown was a brave peace officer in Tascosa. He was so tough that the sheriff had to fire him because he "was always wanting to fight."

Henry found a job on a ranch in northern Oklahoma but soon missed the power of wearing a badge. When a deputy marshal's position opened in nearby Caldwell, Kansas, in July 1882, Henry again became a law officer.

Caldwell was called "The Border Queen," because it was located on the border of Kansas and Oklahoma. It was the toughest town on the famous Chisholm Trail. Several lawmen and a mayor had been killed there.

Caldwell's city marshal was Bat Carr, a Texan who was dangerous with his fists. Deputy Marshal Henry Brown was even more dangerous with his guns. Bat and Henry made a good team of peace officers. They began to establish law and order in Caldwell.

After a few months, Bat Carr returned to Texas. Henry Brown was promoted to city marshal. For his deputy, Henry hired Ben Wheeler, a tall Texan. Wheeler's real name was Ben Robertson, and he was a wanted man in Texas. Henry and Ben made a tough team of lawmen.

On New Year's Day of 1883, citizens of Caldwell presented Marshal Brown a new Winchester. An engraved silver plate on the rifle saluted Henry's "valuable services to the citizens of Caldwell, Kansas."

In May 1883 a Native American named Spotted Horse created a drunken disturbance in Caldwell. As marshal, Henry went after Spotted Horse. He found Spotted Horse in a store and shot him to death with his pistol.

In December 1883 a gambler named Newt Boyce started to cause trouble in town. Henry warned the gambler to behave. One night, Ben Wheeler reported that Boyce was drunk and threatening to kill Henry. Henry grabbed his Winchester and went into the street to find Boyce.

About thirty feet away, Henry spotted Boyce. The gambler reached for a pistol, and Henry shot him in the chest. Boyce died that night.

During the year and a half that Henry was marshal of Caldwell, the only men killed were by Marshal Brown. Henry Brown had tamed Caldwell.

By 1884, Henry was in love. In March 1884 he married Alice Levagood. He bought a house and furniture and a cow for milk. But Henry had to borrow the money to buy these things. Not wanting to be in debt, he decided to rob a bank. Marshal Henry Brown hoped to rob a bank without anyone learning who he was. Ben Wheeler decided to help, and so did two cowboys.

The four captured bank robbers in front of the Medicine Lodge jail. Henry Brown is wearing the light hat and bandanna. Tall Ben Wheeler is at right. That night a lynch mob came to the jail and executed the outlaws.

(Courtesy Kansas State Historical Society)

The bank was in Medicine Lodge, Kansas, about seventy miles west of Caldwell. Henry and Ben Wheeler left town, saying that they were hunting outlaws for a few days. Instead, they met the two cowboys.

On April 30, 1884, the four robbers rode into Medicine Lodge. One of the cowboys held the horses while the other three robbers walked into the bank. The bank president went for a gun, but Henry fired a rifle bullet into his chest. The other two robbers shot the bank cashier.

The robbers ran out of the bank without any money. They galloped out of town, but a posse of angry citizens followed them closely. The outlaws rode into a box canyon, where they were trapped by the posse. After two hours the outlaws were taken back to Medicine Lodge.

Everyone was shocked that the leader of the gang was Marshal Brown. The outlaws were locked inside a log jail. Henry wrote a letter to his bride. He tried to explain that "it was all for you" and that "I did not think this would happen."

Both of the men shot in the bank died. The townspeople decided to lynch the robbers. That night a large mob overpowered the guards. When they opened the jail door, Henry ran past the mob. A farmer blasted him with a shotgun, however, and several other men finished him with rifle bullets.

Ben Wheeler also tried to escape. He was wounded, then taken to a tree. Ben and the other two outlaws were hanged by the lynchers.

Henry Brown had been an outlaw in New Mexico. In Texas and Kansas he became a respected lawman. Only a few weeks after marrying, however, Marshal Brown went bad again. He died at the age of twenty-six.

Jim Miller
"KILLIN' JIM"

"Killin' Jim" Miller was one of the deadliest hired killers in the West. But sometimes he used his guns as a lawman. And Jim enjoyed going to church with his wife so much that he also was called "Deacon Jim."

Jim was raised in Texas, but his parents died when he was a little boy. He lived with his grandparents for a couple of years. When Jim was eight, he murdered his grandparents in their home.

Because he was so young, Jim was sent to live with his sister and her husband, John Coop. But Jim had a bad temper, and he often quarreled with Coop. In 1884, when Jim was seventeen, he shot Coop in the head while he slept.

Jim was tried and convicted of murder, and was sentenced to life in prison. He was set free, however, due to a lawyer's trick.

Jim began working on the ranch of Mannen Clements. In 1887 Clements was shot to death by Joe Townsend, who was the city marshal of Ballinger. Killin' Jim Miller wanted revenge. He took a shotgun and set an ambush near Townsend's house. When Townsend rode home that night, Jim knocked him off his horse with a shotgun blast.

In 1891 Jim married Sallie Clements, daughter of Mannen. Sallie Clements was a Methodist, and Jim went to church with her. Jim seemed to be reforming.

He pinned on a badge as a deputy marshal of Reeves County, in West Texas. Later Jim became city marshal of Pecos, the county seat.

Problems soon arose. When Jim arrested Mexicans, he would shoot them and say that they had tried to escape. Then, in 1894, Sheriff Bud Frazer arrested Jim for stealing a mule. Jim soon was released from jail.

Sheriff Frazer now was afraid of "Killer" Miller. When he saw Jim on the streets of Pecos, he fired a shot without warning. Jim, hit in the right arm, drew his gun with his left hand and opened fire.

But Sheriff Frazer kept shooting. Jim was knocked down by bullets to the chest. Sheriff Frazer thought he had killed Jim. But Jim often wore a steel breastplate under his shirt for protection. The bullets had hit the plate, and Jim soon recovered from his arm wound.

Bud Frazer lost his sheriff's job. He knew he had to kill Jim Miller for his own safety. On the day after Christmas in 1894, Frazer saw Jim standing in a blacksmith shop in Pecos. Frazer suddenly began shooting. Jim was hit in the right arm and left leg. Again he pulled his gun with his left hand and fired back. Frazer shot Jim twice in the chest, but both bullets bounced off Jim's steel plate. Frazer ran away and left Texas for nearby New Mexico.

Killin' Jim waited and watched. Finally, Frazer came out of New Mexico to visit his mother and sister in Toyah, a town near Pecos. Jim traveled to Toyah and found Frazer in a saloon, stuck his shotgun through the saloon door, and blasted Frazer.

Jim was tried for the murder of Sheriff Frazer. Although a man named Joe Earp testified against him, Jim was acquitted. Three weeks after the trial, Jim killed Joe Earp from ambush. Then Jim rode one hundred miles that night to establish an alibi.

Now Jim went back to the other side of the law. He joined the Texas Rangers. For a time he enforced the law in northwest Texas.

In 1900 Jim and his wife moved to Fort Worth. She ran a boardinghouse. And Jim became known as a killer for hire.

In 1902 he shot cattle thieves with his Winchester. One rustler stayed on his horse and escaped. The other two died when shot. A couple of years later, Jim murdered a lawyer near Lubbock. Then he was hired to kill a man named Frank Fore. Jim killed Fore in a Fort Worth hotel. In 1906 Jim was hired to kill a U.S. deputy marshal, Ben Collins of Emet, Oklahoma. Jim ambushed the lawman in front of his house with a shotgun.

When the famous Pat Garrett was murdered in 1908, many people blamed Killin' Jim. As usual, Jim had an alibi.

In 1909 three ranchers near Ada, Oklahoma, hired Killer Miller. They paid him $2,000 to kill another rancher, Gus Bobbitt. Jim ambushed Gus in front of his ranch house. Gus died in the arms of his wife.

While hurrying back to Fort Worth, Jim was arrested and sent back to Ada. The people of Ada were furious over the murder of Gus Bobbitt. A large lynch mob broke into the jail. Jim and the three ranchers were taken to a livery stable and hanged. Jim was forty-two.

He had enforced the law as a deputy sheriff, a city marshal, and a Texas Ranger. But he had murdered people since he was a boy. Killin' Jim Miller is remembered as the number-one assassin in the West.

"Killin' Jim" Miller and the three men who hired him were lynched in a livery stable for the murder of A. A. "Gus" Bobbitt (inset). "Killer" Miller is at left, wearing a hat.

(Courtesy Western History Collections, University of Oklahoma Library)

Tom Horn was a hero of the Old West who later became a hired killer.
(Courtesy Arizona Historical Society)

Tom Horn
LAWMAN AND HIRED KILLER

Tom Horn was an adventurous farm boy from Missouri who wanted to go west. Tom ran away from home when he was fourteen. He drove a wagon on the Santa Fe Trail, drove a stagecoach, and became a cowboy.

In Arizona Tom signed on with the army as a scout. For several years he served as a scout during the Apache wars. Tom was with the army in 1886, when Geronimo became the last chief to surrender.

When the army no longer needed scouts, Tom became a deputy sheriff in Yavapai County, Arizona. In 1890 he joined the Pinkerton Detective Agency. As a Pinkerton detective, Tom headquartered in Denver for the next four years.

In 1894 Tom was hired by Wyoming ranchers to halt cattle theft. Rustlers were stealing great numbers of cattle from the big ranches. The ranchers wanted Tom Horn to track down the rustlers. Tom had tracked Apaches for the U.S. Army. He had hunted outlaws as a deputy sheriff and as a Pinkerton detective. The ranchers knew he would be an excellent stock detective.

Horn rode the ranges constantly. In 1895 a man named William Lewis bragged about stealing cattle. Lewis was warned to leave the country. When he did not leave, he was shot to death on the range. Lewis was killed with three rifle bullets from a distance of 300 yards. Everyone thought that Tom Horn had killed Lewis.

Fred Powell, a rustler who had helped William Lewis, also was warned to leave Wyoming. Instead, he invited cowboys to eat a meal of stolen beef. Then a rider shot Powell to death. The killer was a big man, like Tom Horn.

Tom enjoyed drinking and talking in saloons. He began to brag about his deadly reputation. Rustlers began to leave the country.

In 1898 the United States entered a war against Spain over Cuba. Tom again felt a call to adventure and duty. He joined the army as a teamster.

When the war ended, Tom returned to Wyoming and went back to work as a stock detective for the big ranches. Tom learned that many rustlers hid out in Brown's Park, a rugged area in northwestern Colorado. He decided to ride into Brown's Park.

Within three months Tom killed two rustlers. On July 8, 1900, Matt Rash stepped outside his cabin and was hit by three rifle bullets. On October 3 a black cowboy named Isom Dart was struck by two rifle bullets fired from a distance of 200 yards.

The next year Tom was suspected of the murder of fourteen-year-old Willie Nickell. Willie's father, Kels Nickell, had a small ranch near the big ranch of John Coble, one of Tom Horn's employers. Coble suspected Kels of rustling. Kels once had stabbed Coble. Kels also had brought a flock of sheep to his ranch, which angered all of the cattle ranchers in the area. Kels had trouble with his neighbors, the Miller family. Willie Nickell had a fight with one of the Miller boys.

Willie was killed while opening a ranch gate on July 18, 1901. Because it was a rainy day, he was wearing his father's hat and coat. Perhaps the killer had mistaken Willie for his father. Willie was shot at long range by a rifle.

At first most people thought that the Millers had killed Willie. But Tom Horn had been seen riding the range nearby. Then people began to think that John Coble might have hired Tom to kill Kels Nickell.

A detective named Joe LeFors asked Tom to have a talk. Tom did not know that two more men were in the next room. LeFors began to ask

Tom about the Nickell killing. Although Tom bragged about his skill as a rifle shot, he never admitted to killing Willie Nickell.

But Joe LeFors claimed that what Tom had said amounted to a confession. Tom was arrested and tried for murder in Cheyenne, Wyoming. The big ranchers hired famous lawyers to defend Tom. But most of the twelve jury members were small ranchers. They hated the big ranchers and their hired killer, Tom Horn. The jury chose to believe the "confession" (the LeFors "confession" would not be permitted in a modern court).

The jury found Tom guilty of murder. Even if Tom did not murder Willie, he had indeed killed many other men.

Two months before he was scheduled to hang, Tom escaped from the Cheyenne jail. He was quickly captured and put back in jail.

Tom was hanged on November 20, 1903, the day before his forty-third birthday. He faced death with great courage. Of course, Tom had been brave all of his life. In the West he had shown his courage as an army scout, deputy sheriff, detective, and soldier. But many people forgot Tom's brave deeds after he became a hired killer.

The courthouse and jail where Tom Horn was confined, tried, and hanged. The courtroom was on the second floor, the jail at the rear.

(Courtesy Wyoming State Archives, Museums and Historical Department)

Western Words

alias—an outlaw sometimes would use an **alias**, or a different name. An **alias** of Billy the Kid was William Bonney; an **alias** of Jesse James was Thomas Howard.

alibi—criminals, such as "Killin' Jim" Miller, often tried to create an **alibi**, a story that would place them somewhere else when a crime was committed.

assassin—a hired killer who murdered, or **assassinated**, victims without warning.

bounty hunter—a cash reward, or bounty, often was paid for the capture of an outlaw. A man who hunted outlaws for pay was a **bounty hunter**.

buckshot—small lead balls that were fired from a shotgun.

bushwhacker—a bushwhacker tried to kill from **ambush**. The bushwhacker would shoot an unsuspecting victim from a hiding place.

constable—a lawman who worked for a town.

derringer—a small pistol used as a hideout gun. A **derringer** usually had one or two short barrels that fired one shot apiece.

desperado—an outlaw who was desperate to escape from lawmen.

double-barreled shotgun—many gunfighters used a **shotgun**, which fired a powerful blast of **buckshot**. Shotguns usually had two barrels, so a double blast of buckshot could be fired.

fugitive—a man running from the law; an **outlaw**.

heeled—a man who carried a gun was considered **heeled**.

marshal—a city **marshal** was the head peace officer of a Western town; today he would be called the **chief of police**. An **assistant marshal** worked for the city marshal. A **U.S. marshal** was the chief law officer of a large district. Many **deputy marshals** worked for the U.S. marshal.

Pinkerton detective—The **Pinkerton Detective Agency** investigated crimes all over the West. A **Pinkerton** man worked for the most famous detective agency in the West.

revolver—a revolver was a **pistol**, or **handgun**, which could fire six bullets. Invented by Sam Colt, this weapon often was called a **six-gun**.

sheriff—a sheriff was the chief law officer of a county. **Deputy sheriffs** worked for the sheriff.

teamster—a man who drove a team of mules, horses, or oxen. Cargo was packed onto the animals, or the animals pulled a wagon filled with cargo.

vigilante—citizens who were afraid that outlaws would escape justice. **Vigilantes** would capture outlaws, then **lynch** them. A **lynch mob** usually hanged outlaws.

Winchester—the most popular rifle in the West. The **Winchester** could be fired rapidly by cocking a lever behind the trigger.

Places to Visit

Tombstone, Arizona—The West's most famous shootout, the Gunfight at the O.K. Corral, happened in Tombstone. So did many other gunfights. The O.K. Corral still stands in Tombstone. Men dressed as the Earps, Clantons, McLaurys, and Doc Holliday often act out the O.K. Corral fight for tourists.

Lincoln, New Mexico—Lincoln has changed very little from the 1870s, when it was the center of the Lincoln County War. Billy the Kid shot his way out of the two-story courthouse. Lincoln is one of the great gunfighter towns of the West.

Fort Sumner, New Mexico—There are many ruins of the old community where Billy the Kid was killed by Pat Garrett. Tom O'Folliard was killed at Fort Sumner by Garrett's posse. Billy the Kid killed Joe Grant in a Fort Sumner saloon. Billy is buried in the old cemetery beside his pals, Tom O'Folliard and Charlie Bowdre.

Texas Ranger Hall of Fame—This exciting Texas Ranger museum is in Waco, Texas. The magnificent firearm collection includes guns owned by many famous Rangers, Tom Horn, and other important gunfighters.

Jesse James House—The little house where the legendary outlaw was killed is in St. Joseph, Missouri. Not far to the south, the James Farm and Jesse's grave may be visited.

Cody, Wyoming—The Buffalo Bill Historical Center displays 5,000 frontier rifles and pistols. The Old Trail Town and Museum of the Old West includes a log cabin used as a hideout by Butch Cassidy and the Sundance Kid.

Old Abilene Town—A reconstruction of the first Kansas cowtown, where Wild Bill Hickok killed Phil Coe.

Dodge City, Kansas—Wyatt Earp and Bat Masterson were lawmen here, and many other famous fights took place in Dodge. The most important block of the old cowtown has been reconstructed.

Bibliography

Many books have been written about Western gunfighters. Biographies tell the life stories of most of the gunfighters. The books that have the most information are written for adults, but young readers as well can learn more about gunfighters from many of these sources.

Books about Gunfighters and Gunfighting

O'Neal, Bill. *Encyclopedia of Western Gunfighters*. Norman: University of Oklahoma Press, 1979.
Rosa, Joseph G. *Age of the Gunfighter*. Norman: University of Oklahoma Press, 1993.
———. *The Gunfighter, Man or Myth?* Norman: University of Oklahoma Press, 1969.
Trachtman, Paul. *The Gunfighters*. New York: Time-Life Books, 1974.

BILLY THE KID
Bell, Bob Boze. *The Illustrated Life and Times of Billy the Kid*. Phoeniz, AZ: Tri-Star-Boze Publications, Inc., 1996.
Nolan, Frederick. *The Lincoln County War*. Norman: University of Oklahoma Press, 1992.
Rasch, Philip J. *Trailing Billy the Kid*. Stillwater, OK: National Association for Outlaw and Lawman History, Inc., 1995.
Utley, Robert M. *Billy the Kid, A Short and Violent Life*. Lincoln: University of Nebraska Press, 1989.

HENRY BROWN
O'Neal, Bill. *Henry Brown, The Outlaw Marshal*. College Station, TX: Creative Publishing Company, 1980.

WYATT EARP
Bell, Bob Boze. *The Illustrated Life and Times of Wyatt Earp*. Phoenix, AZ: Tri Star-Boze Publications, Inc., 1995.

Hickey, Michael M. *Street Fight in Tombstone, Near the O.K. Corral*. Published by Michael M. Hickey, 1991.

Tefertiller, Casey. *Wyatt Earp, The Life Behind the Legend*. New York: John Wiley & Sons, Inc., 1997.

PAT GARRETT

Metz, Leon C. *Pat Garrett: The Story of a Western Lawman*. Norman: University of Oklahoma Press, 1974.

WES HARDIN

Marohn, Richard C. *The Last Gunfighter, John Wesley Hardin*. College Station, TX: The Early West, 1995.

WILD BILL HICKOK

Fiedler, Mildred. *Wild Bill and Deadwood*. New York: Bonanza Books, 1965.

Rosa, Joseph G. *They Called Him Wild Bill: The Life and Adventures of James Butler Hickok*. Norman: University of Oklahoma Press, 1964.

———. *The West of Wild Bill Hickok*. Norman: University of Oklahoma Press, 1982.

DOC HOLLIDAY

Jahns, Pat. *The Frontier World of Doc Holliday*. Lincoln: University of Nebraska Press, 1957.

Tanner, Karen Holliday. *Doc Holliday, A Family Portrait*. Norman: University of Oklahoma Press, 1998.

Traywick, Ben T. *John Henry (The "Doc" Holliday Story)*. Tombstone: Red Marie's Bookstore, 1996.

TOM HORN

Carlson, Chip. *Tom Horn, "Killing Men is My Specialty."* Cheyenne: Beartooth Corral, 1991.

Krakel, Dean F. *The Saga of Tom Horn*. Lincoln: University of Nebraska Press, 1954.

Nunis, Doyce B., Jr. *The Life of Tom Horn Revisited*. San Marino, CA: The Westerners Los Angeles Corral, 1992.

JOHN HUGHES

Martin, Jack. *Border Boss*. San Antonio: Naylor Company, 1942.

Webb, Walter P. *The Texas Rangers*. Austin: University of Texas Press, 1935.

JESSE JAMES

Baldwin, Margaret, and Pat O'Brien. *Wanted! Frank & Jesse James, The Real Story*. New York: Julian Messner, 1981.

Settle, William A., Jr. *Jesse James Was His Name*. Columbia, MO: University of Missouri Press, 1966.

Steele, Phillip W., with George Warfel. *The Many Faces of Jesse James*. Gretna, LA: Pelican Publishing Company, 1995.

HARVEY LOGAN

Baker, Pearl. *The Wild Bunch at Robbers Roost*. New York: Abelard-Schuman, Ltd., 1965.

Horan, James D., and Paul Sann. *Pictorial History of the Wild West*. New York: Crown Publishers, Inc., 1954.

BAT MASTERSON

DeArment, Robert K. *Bat Masterson, The Man and the Legend*. Norman: University of Oklahoma Press, 1979.

Masterson, Bat. *Famous Gunfighters of the Western Frontier*. Published in *Human Life Magazine*, 1907.

JIM MILLER

Shirley, Glenn. *Shotgun for Hire: The Story of "Deacon" Jim Miller, Killer of Pat Garrett*. Norman: University of Oklahoma Press, 1970.

JIM ROBERTS

O'Neal, Bill. *Cattlemen vs. Sheepherders*. Austin: Eakin Press, 1989.

Trimble, Marshall. *Arizona Adventure*. Phoenix: Golden West Publishers, 1982.

JOHN SELMAN

Metz, Leon C. *John Selman: Texas Gunfighter*. New York: Hastings House Publishers, 1966.

DALLAS STOUDENMIRE

Metz, Leon C. *Dallas Stoudenmire: El Paso Marshal*. Austin: Pemberton Press, 1969.

HECK THOMAS

Shirley, Glenn. *Heck Thomas, Frontier Marshal*. Philadelphia: Chilton Company, 1962.

BEN THOMPSON

Paine, Lauran. *Texas Ben Thompson*. Los Angeles: Westernlore Press, 1966.

Schoenberger, Dale T. *The Gunfighters*. Caldwell, ID: Caxton Printers, Ltd., 1971.

Streeter, Floyd B. *Ben Thompson, Man with a Gun*. New York: Frederick Fell, Inc., 1957.

HARRY WHEELER

O'Neal, Bill. *The Arizona Rangers*. Austin: Eakin Press, 1987.

COLE YOUNGER

Brant, Marley. *Outlaws: The Illustrated History of the James-Younger Gang*. Montgomery, AL: Elliott & Clark, 1997.

———. *The Outlaw Youngers: A Confederate Brotherhood: A Biography*. Lanham, MD: Madison Books, 1995.

About the Author

BILL O'NEAL'S great-grandfather was a Texas cowboy, and his grandmother came to Texas in a covered wagon when she was a little girl in 1881. When Bill was a boy growing up in Texas, he learned to love the West by going to Western movies.

Bill now teaches Western history at Panola College in Carthage, Texas. He has written more than twenty books about Western history and baseball. His books have covered ghost towns, gunfighters, and cattle ranches. One of his books is about Singing Cowboy movie star Tex Ritter. Bill's next book will be about the famous Western singing group, the Sons of the Pioneers.